Written by Pamela Hickman • Illustrated by Heather Collins

THE KIDS CANADIAN

Plant

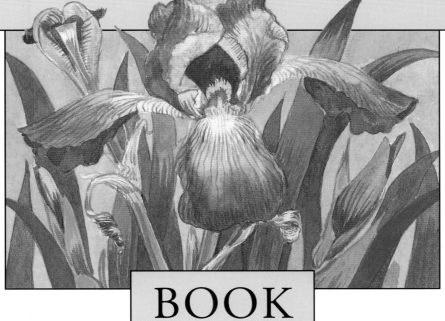

BOOK

Kids Can Press

Kids Can Press acknowledges the financial support of the Ontario Arts Council, the Canada Council for the Arts and the Government of Canada, through BPIDP, for our publishing activity.

Published in Canada by
Kids Can Press Ltd.
29 Birch Avenue
Toronto, ON M4V 1E2

www.kidscanpress.com

Edited by Trudee Romanek
Series editor: Laurie Wark
Designed by Blair Kerrigan/Glyphics

Printed in Hong Kong, China
by Wing King Tong Company Limited

The hardcover edition of this book is smyth sewn casebound.
The paperback edition of this book is limp sewn with a drawn-on cover.

CDN 97 0 9 8 7 6 5 4 3 2
CM PA 97 0 9 8 7 6 5 4 3 2

Canadian Cataloguing in Publication Data

Hickman, Pamela
    The kids Canadian plant book

Includes index.
ISBN 1-55074-233-7 (bound)
ISBN 1-55074-331-7 (pbk.)

1. Plants — Juvenile literature. 2. Botany — Canada — Juvenile literature. I. Collins, Heather. II Title.

QK201.H53 1995   j581.971   C95-931857-7

Acknowledgements

Many thanks to the wonderful staff at Kids Can Press for their help with this book. I'd also like to thank my many gardening friends over the years who have shared their knowledge, and plants, so freely.

For Ashley, Adam and Alexander Hickman
PH

Kids Can Press is a *l'orus*™ Entertainment company

CONTENTS

Meet a plant

Do you have plants in a garden, or on your balcony? Are there flowers growing in pots on your windowsill or arranged in a vase of water? No matter where you live in Canada you'll find many different plants. Woodlands, fields, prairies, mountains, wetlands and shorelines are all homes to a great variety of wildflowers, grasses and much more. You'll find plants growing in crowded cities, along fences and even through sidewalk cracks. Wherever they grow, they provide food and shelter for wildlife, help keep soil from being washed away, and give off oxygen that animals need to breathe.

They may also help to clean water in streams and rivers, and provide people with food, medicines and materials for clothing and crafts.

Plants can be divided into two groups: nonflowering and flowering. Nonflowering plants include ferns, mosses and other plants that reproduce by spores instead of seeds. This book looks at flowering plants, which includes most of the plants you see around you.

Plant parts

All flowering plants have four basic parts: roots, stems, leaves and flowers. The roots suck up from the soil water and minerals that the plant needs to grow. The stem supports the plant. Inside the stem are tiny tubes that carry water and food to all parts of the plant. A plant's leaves are like tiny factories. They use carbon dioxide from the air and water and sunlight to produce sugars, which the plant uses as food. This process is called photosynthesis. Flowers are important because they produce seeds. Seeds in turn grow into new plants.

flowering plant

flower

leaves

stem

roots

Trees

Trees are also a kind of plant. They have thick, woody stems and grow much bigger than the soft-stemmed plants in this book. Like most plants, trees have roots, stems and leaves or needles. Most trees also have flowers.

What plants need to grow

You need food and water in order to grow and stay healthy, and so do plants. They get water and minerals from the soil and make food in their leaves during photosynthesis. In order to make food, plants must have sunlight and warm temperatures. In tropical countries, where the climate is warmer and wetter than in Canada, many kinds of plants grow much bigger than they do here.

A GROWING CONCERN

Find out how important sunlight and water are with this experiment.

You'll need:

three small, potted, flowering plants of the same kind

a dark closet

a sunny window

water

1. Put one plant in a dark closet and the other two in a sunny window.

2. Do not water one of the plants in the window for two weeks, but water the others regularly.

3. After two weeks, put all three plants side-by-side and compare them.

The plant without water will be wilting, and some of its leaves may be yellow or dead. When they are full of water, the tiny tubes inside the plant's stems, leaves and flower stalks are strong and stiff. If there isn't enough water, they become limp and droop, or wilt. Eventually the plant cuts off the water supply to its leaves and flowers, and they drop off. If the plant dries out completely, it will die.

When a plant is kept in the dark, its leaves turn yellow and stop making food, and the plant becomes weaker. The plant that received both water and sunlight should be healthy and growing well.

After you have looked at your plants, put them all in the window and nurse the weak ones back to health.

plant with sunlight and water

plant with water, but no sunlight

plant with sunlight, but no water

Pollination

Take a look at the flowers in your neighbourhood. You'll see a rainbow of colours and lots of different shapes and sizes. If you get nose-to-nose with some flowers, you can smell their sweet scents.

The **pistil** is made up of the stigma, style and ovary.

anther

filament

The **stamen** is made up of the filament and anther.

pollen grains on anther

petal

sepal

stigma

style

egg cells inside ovary

People have enjoyed flowers for thousands of years, but the colours, shapes and fragrances of flowers are really designed to attract birds, bats or insects such as Honey Bees, not people.

Flowers must be pollinated to produce seeds that will grow into new plants. Pollination means that pollen from a flower lands on its own stigma or the stigma of another flower of the same kind. Flowers are pollinated by wind and animals.

Some flowers are specially designed to attract animal pollinators. These flowers are usually large and have a special shape, colour or scent. Sometimes they are made up of many tiny flowers clumped together, like a dandelion. The pollen grains are large and sticky, so they collect on the pollinator's body hairs, legs or feathers. When the animal visits another flower, the pollen gets rubbed off and pollinates that flower.

POLLINATE A FLOWER

Like a Honey Bee, you can pollinate a flower. Then keep watch over the next few weeks as your flower makes its seeds. If you collect the seeds later, when they are dry, you can plant them in your garden next year and grow many new plants, with lots more flowers.

You'll need:

a tiny paintbrush

a small piece of cardboard

some coloured yarn

1. Find a patch of flowers, all the same kind, that have just opened. Rub your finger lightly on the anthers. If some pollen comes off on your finger, the flowers are ready to be pollinated.

2. With your paintbrush, gently collect some pollen from the anthers of a flower and brush it onto your cardboard.

3. Move to another flower and paint its stigma with the pollen on the cardboard.

4. Tie a piece of coloured yarn loosely around the bottom of the flower, where it is attached to the stem. This marker will help you remember which flower you pollinated.

5. Pollinate several flowers, but use only the pollen that comes from the same kind of flower.

Surviving winter

One of the most exciting things about spring is discovering tiny green shoots poking through the soil where the snow has just melted. How do plants survive icy-cold winters? Like many animals, plants hibernate, or rest, during winter. When the killing frosts of fall arrive, the above-ground stems and flowers of most plants die. Annuals, like marigolds and petunias, die completely in the cold. Perennials — plants that come back year after year, such as Wild Carrot and trilliums — don't die completely. Instead, perennials have underground roots or bulbs that survive the winter and send up new shoots when the warm weather returns. Some plants also leave a ring, or rosette, of ground-hugging leaves under the snow. The new growth sprouts up through these leaves in spring.

Wildflowers produce seeds that fall to the ground and spend winter safe inside their tough seed coats. When warm weather thaws the ground, the seeds soak up water from the soil until they burst their seed coats and shoots and roots grow out. Soon they will become new plants.

Winter wildflowers

Look for the dried stalks of these winter wildflowers in open fields or along roadsides and fence rows.

dock

Wild Carrot

Teasel

goldenrod

Search for spring

In late winter, visit some woods or a field and look for plants under the snow. If the dried stems of last year's plants are still standing, use a trowel to carefully dig the snow away from the base to find the rosette of overwintering leaves. Check areas where you saw wildflowers blooming last season. When you've finished peeking at the resting flowers, cover them back up with snow to protect them from the cold. Make a note of where they are and go back in the spring to see what has grown. If you record the location of other wildflowers you find in the spring, you'll be able to find them more easily next winter.

Evening Primrose

milkweed

thistle

mullein

Common Tansy

Rosette

Grow a winter garden

If you look outside and see nothing but ice and snow, summer can seem a long way off. This winter, start things growing early by planting a vegetable garden indoors. Potatoes, sweet potatoes, carrots, parsnips and onions are all good choices. They have lots of food energy stored in them to help new plants grow.

You'll need:

carrots, parsnips or onions that have sprouted green leaves, or potatoes with eyes

a knife

15 cm–20 cm pots or plastic containers with holes in the bottom for drainage, one container for each vegetable

potting soil

1. Ask an adult to cut the carrots, parsnips or potatoes so that each green sprout or eye has a piece of vegetable attached that is at least 3 cm thick.

2. Fill each pot with potting soil and keep the soil damp, but not soaking. Plant each sprout so that the vegetable is buried and the sprout is above the soil. Potato eyes should be buried completely.

3. Place your pots in a sunny window and watch your winter garden grow.

4. In the spring, carefully dig up your potted vegetables to see what has happened in the soil. The plant should have new roots, and the original vegetable has likely shrunk, since its stored food was used to produce the new plant.

5. Plant your vegetables outdoors in a garden or in large pots after the last spring frost.

Onions
An onion is a bulb that stores food for the plant underground. You can snip off some of the green leaves and add them to sandwiches and salads.

Potatoes
An ordinary potato grows into a tall, leafy plant, and a sweet potato grows into a beautiful vine. Your plant should produce some new potatoes to eat.

Carrots and parsnips
The carrots and parsnips that you eat are really big roots called tap roots. Your plant will produce seeds that you can use to grow new plants.

13

Plants across Canada

Canada is made up of many different habitats. Each one has a special climate and soils that suit the plants that grow there. Read on to find out how plants are adapted to grow in your part of the country.

Arctic and alpine plants

Plants in the Arctic and alpine plants high up in the mountains both face cold, dry and often windy climates and a short growing season. To survive, they must grow very quickly, produce flowers, be pollinated, and make seeds before they are killed by early frosts. They grow very close to the ground, often huddled together in clumps, to keep out of the wind. Their leaves are sometimes hairy or woolly to cut down on water loss and to provide insulation from the cold.

Prairie plants

Prairie wildflowers and grasses are well adapted to deal with low rainfall and strong winds. When the stems and leaves of the plants die each fall, the dead vegetation forms a thick layer over the ground. This helps to keep the soil from drying out or blowing away. Prairie grasses have thick roots that spread and intertwine with each other to form a kind of mat, which also helps to hold the soil in place.

Woodland plants

In the spring, plants on the forest floor grow quickly while the sunlight can reach them. Before long, the leaves of the trees will come out and shade everything below. Woodland wildflowers, such as trilliums and Spring-beauty, have only a few weeks to grow, flower, make seeds, and store enough food in their underground roots or bulbs for next year's growth. After a long winter, insect pollinators, such as bees, rely on these early plants for food.

Aquatic plants

Aquatic plants don't have to worry about running out of water. They are surrounded by it! Their challenge is to get air to their waterlogged roots. Water-lilies have channels in their long, flexible stems to carry air to the underwater roots. Most plants have their stomata (tiny holes where air and water pass in and out) on the underside of their leaves to reduce water loss. But the floating leaves of water-lilies have their stomata on top so the plant can get more air. Many underwater plants, such as water-milfoils, have leaves that are divided into many tiny parts so they can move easily in the water currents without being torn.

Starting with seeds

A seed is like a tiny picnic basket full of food that the plant uses when it starts to grow. Before a seed can sprout, or germinate, it must have water. In the winter the water in the ground is frozen and seeds can't use it. In the spring the ice thaws and the seeds begin to sprout. They soak up water like sponges until they get so big that they burst. A tiny root and a shoot poke out of each seed. They will grow into a new plant if they get enough food from the soil and enough water and sunlight.

There are two kinds of flowering plants: monocots and dicots. The seed of a monocot contains a large store of food, called an endosperm, and one seed leaf, or cotyledon. When the seed sprouts, a root and only one leaf grow out of it. Grass is an example of a monocot. A dicot stores its food in two seed leaves. They pop out of the seed, along with the growing root, when the seed germinates. As the plant uses up the stored food to grow bigger, the two seed leaves shrivel up. Most garden flowers, fruits and vegetables are dicots.

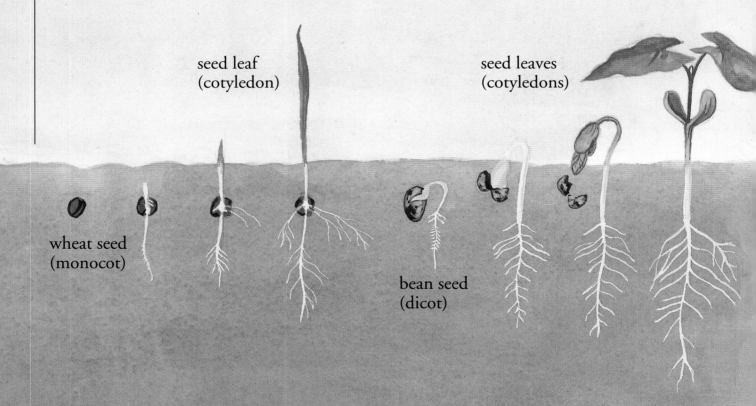

seed leaf (cotyledon)

seed leaves (cotyledons)

wheat seed (monocot)

bean seed (dicot)

SPROUT SOME SEEDS

You can watch corn and bean seeds sprout and compare monocot and dicot seedlings. If you do this activity in the spring, you can transplant your sprouts outdoors. Bean sprouts are also delicious to eat in salads and sandwiches any time of year.

You'll need:

some corn seed and mung beans

water

a bowl

paper towels

two glass jars

1. Soak your seeds in a bowl of water overnight to speed up germination.

2. Line the jars with paper towels folded in half. Add a few centimetres of water. In one jar, place some corn seeds between the paper towel and the glass. Put mung beans in the other jar in the same way.

3. Keep the paper towels damp. Over the next few days, watch the seeds swell as they soak up the water.

4. Compare the seeds when they germinate and the roots and shoots appear. How many seed leaves does the corn have? And the beans? Which seeds are monocots and which are dicots?

Spreading seeds

In order to grow, a seed must land where it will have enough soil, water and sunshine. Some seeds sail on the wind, float in the water or hitch a ride on an animal to move away from the plant that produced them. Others explode or catapult right out of their seed pods! It is very important for seeds to spread out so that plants can grow in new areas. Overcrowding causes seeds to compete for soil nutrients and water, and not all the plants can survive.

Many seeds don't land in the right spot, so they never grow. Some flowers produce thousands of seeds, so there is a better chance at least some of them will survive and grow into new plants. Discover how the seeds of these common wildflowers are spread.

You probably love to eat the sweet red fruits of wild strawberry, and so do other animals. The tiny seeds on the berries are hard to digest, so they are excreted in the animals' waste, often a long way from where the berries were growing. This is how strawberry seeds get "planted" in new areas.

Jewelweed, also called touch-me-not, grows in damp woodlands. In late summer, look for a long, narrow, bulging seed pod and gently squeeze it between your thumb and first finger. The seed pod immediately bursts and coils up, throwing the seeds through the air.

Look for milkweed in dry open fields and roadsides in late summer and early fall. When the large, fat pods are ripe, they split and release the seeds to the wind. Each little brown seed is attached to a parachutelike bit of fluff that carries it through the air, sometimes over long distances. Blow on some seeds to send them on their way.

If you or your pet wander through open fields in the fall, you may find the prickly seeds of burdock stuck to your clothing or in your pet's fur. The seed cases, or burs, are covered with hooks that catch on passing animals, helping the seeds to hitch a ride to a new growing place. When animals try to pull the burs out of their fur, the seed cases split and the seeds spill out.

Plant defences

If you are in danger, you can run away or hide. Have you ever wondered how plants defend themselves from enemies, such as plant-eating animals? The prickles on thistles, the thorns on roses and the spikes on Teasel are all ways of discouraging plant eaters. They may keep people away too.

You can *see* prickles and thorns, but some plant defences are harder to spot. Stinging Nettles have tiny, needlelike hairs on their leaves. The hairs are filled with a liquid that stings when it gets on your skin. Once you've been stung by nettles you quickly learn to recognize them and stay away.

Another plant to avoid on hikes or at the cottage is Poison Ivy. This woody vine or shrub grows in woodlands and along fences in the country. Look for its three leaves and, in the fall, its white berries. The plant's sap causes a very itchy and uncomfortable rash on your skin, so don't touch the plant or its berries.

Stinging Nettles

thistle

Teasel

Wild rose

Poison Ivy
For Poison Ivy, remember this rhyme:
*"Leaves three, let it be.
Berries white, take
flight."*

Poisonous plants

Munching on wild raspberries or chewing wood-sorrel can be fun when you're on a hike or at the cottage, but it is dangerous to eat wild plants unless you are absolutely sure what they are. **Always check with an adult before eating wild plants.** Some plants are very poisonous to people and can easily be mistaken for harmless plants. For instance, not all berries are good to eat. The bright red berries of Bittersweet Nightshade, Red Baneberry, American Yew and Red-berried Elder are poisonous and should never be eaten. The seeds of common flowers such as lupines, larkspurs, Monkshood and sweet peas are also very poisonous. Even some garden plants can be dangerous; although the stems of rhubarb are delicious when cooked, the leaves are poisonous.

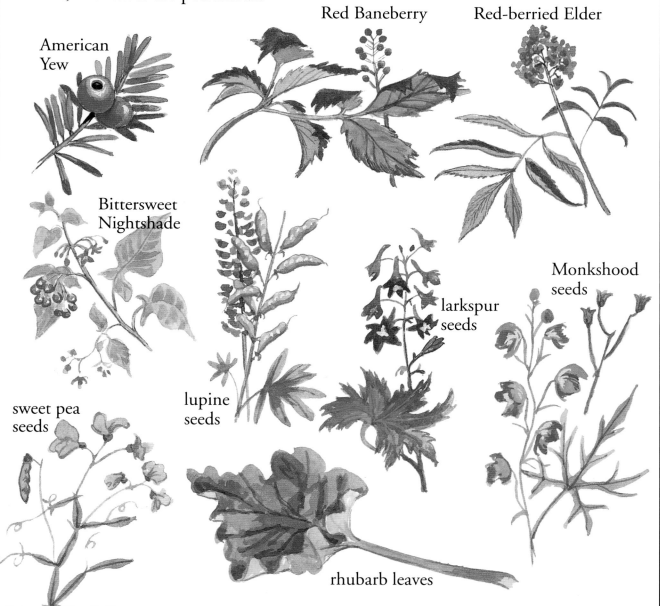

American Yew

Red Baneberry

Red-berried Elder

Bittersweet Nightshade

Monkshood seeds

larkspur seeds

sweet pea seeds

lupine seeds

rhubarb leaves

Looking at lawns

Have you ever wondered what your lawn would look like if the grass was never cut? To find out, ask an adult to help you fence off a small area with string and tall sticks or garden stakes. When the lawn is cut, ask that your special area be left alone. The hollow stems and long leaves of the grass will soon reach above your knees. Eventually, tiny greenish or yellowish flowers will appear at the top of the stems. Since grass is pollinated by the wind, it doesn't need large or colourful flowers to attract pollinators. The wind blows the pollen from one flower to another, and tiny grass seeds form.

A close-up look at your lawn

Many lawns and playgrounds have more than just grass growing in them. Find out what's growing in your lawn, school yard or park with this simple activity. Lay a Hula Hoop, or a string tied in a circle, on the grass. Get down on your hands and knees and look closely at the plants within the circle. Use a magnifying glass, if you have one. How many different kinds of plants do you see? Compare their leaves and stems. Do they grow straight up or along the ground? Look for insects and other tiny creatures that live in the grass, too.

Plants and you

When you go for a walk in a field or forest, you will see all kinds of plants. They provide food and shelter for a variety of wildlife ranging in size from tiny insects to huge moose. Even meat eaters, such as foxes, rely on plants, because the rabbits and mice they eat need plants for food. Without plants, there would be no animals.

The roots of plants are important because they hold the soil in place. Plant leaves also help protect soil by sheltering it from heavy rains and strong winds that could carry it away. Wetland plants, such as cattails, help to keep rivers and streams clean by trapping sediment and absorbing pollution from the water.

Provincial flowers

Which flower represents your province or territory?

1.	Yukon	Fireweed
2.	Northwest Territories	Mountain Avens
3.	British Columbia	Pacific Dogwood
4.	Alberta	Wild Rose
5.	Saskatchewan	Western Red Lily
6.	Manitoba	Prairie Crocus
7.	Ontario	White Trillium
8.	Quebec	White Garden Lily (Madonna Lily)
9.	New Brunswick	Purple Violet
10.	Nova Scotia	Mayflower (Trailing Arbutus)
11.	Prince Edward Island	Lady's-slipper
12.	Newfoundland	Pitcher-plant

9.

5.

10.

People rely on plants for food and medicine. For thousands of years people have used herbal (plant) remedies for a variety of problems, including toothaches and fevers. The cures for some types of cancer, heart disease and other serious illnesses have been made from plants. Cloth, such as cotton and linen, and craft materials, such as straw and reeds, also come from plants.

People often use plants in their celebrations. How many plants can you think of that are used for special occasions?

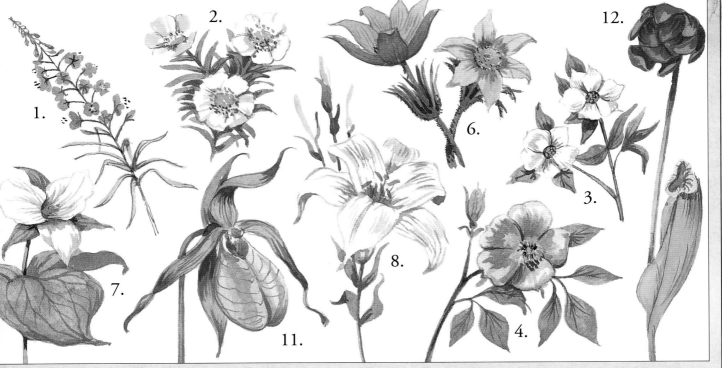

1.

2.

3.

4.

6.

7.

8.

11.

12.

Endangered plants

When a meadow is ploughed under, a forest is cut down or a marsh is filled in, the plants that live in these habitats are destroyed. Habitat loss is the main reason some plants are endangered. Other causes of endangerment include the overpicking of certain flowers, especially orchids, and the invasion by new plants that aren't naturally found in a certain habitat. Purple Loosestrife is an example of a flowering plant from Europe that was accidentally introduced into North American marshes. It is taking over the habitats, and other marsh plants are dying out. When plant species die out, the animals that depend on these plants also suffer.

Canada's endangered plants

When a species becomes endangered it must be helped or it may become extinct. (Extinction means there are no more of those plants growing anywhere in the world.) More than 20 species of plants are listed as endangered in Canada. They include the Pink Coreopsis and the Eastern Mountain Avens of Nova Scotia, Ontario's Small White Lady's-slipper, Spotted Wintergreen, and Prickly Pear Cactus.

Eastern Mountain Avens

Spotted Wintergreen

Prickly Pear cactus

Purple Loosestrife

Small White
Lady's-slipper

Pink
Coreopsis

You can help

Some plants are protected by laws. Others are kept safe in national and provincial parks and nature reserves. You can also help protect plants and their habitats.

- Tell your family and friends why plants are important in nature.

- Enjoy wild plants in their natural habitats instead of picking them or digging them up to bring home.

- Stay on paths and hiking trails in parks so you don't trample nearby plants.

- Help take care of the plants in your yard, at school or at the cottage.

- Raise money for conservation groups that protect native plants and their habitats.

How does your garden grow?

If you live in Victoria, B.C., your garden will grow earlier and last longer than a garden in northern New Brunswick. That's because different regions of Canada have different climates. Canada is divided into ten main growing zones based on their climates. The map below shows the zones, but some are small and might be hard to see. Check a detailed gardening catalogue to find out exactly which growing zone you live in and which plants will grow best in your area.

GROW SOME VEGETABLES

If you have a yard or a sunny space for some large flowerpots, you can plant some vegetables in the spring and even grow your own Hallowe'en pumpkin.

You'll need:

one package each of radish, pea and pumpkin seeds

gardening tools, such as a rake, a shovel and a trowel

sticks about the size of a pencil

watering can

flowerpots and potting soil (optional)

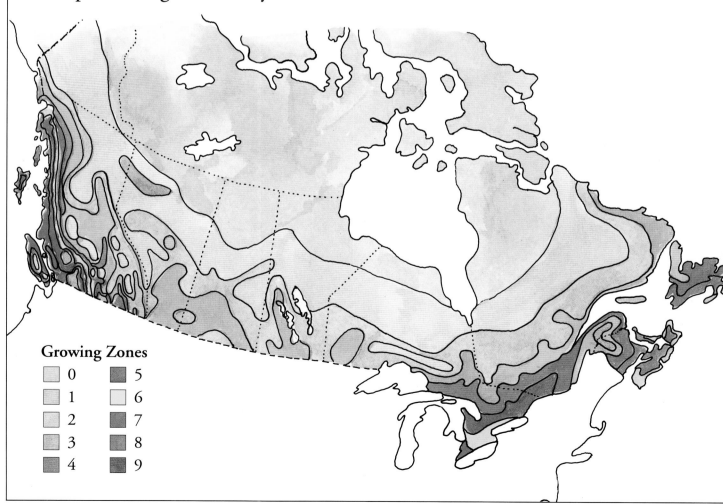

Growing Zones

- 0
- 1
- 2
- 3
- 4
- 5
- 6
- 7
- 8
- 9

1. Dig a garden 1 m x 1 m in a sunny spot with good drainage, or fill your flowerpots with potting soil.

2. Plant your seeds. Follow the directions on each seed package.

3. Attach the empty seed packages to sticks and use them to label your rows or pots.

4. Water your garden when it is dry and pull out the weeds. Weeds take food and moisture out of the soil and away from your growing vegetables.

Climbing peas need support, so "plant" some sticks in your row of peas. The sticks should be 1 m high and have several branches coming out of them. The pea vines will climb up the sticks instead of flopping on the ground. When the pods feel fat, about 60 days after planting, the peas inside are ready to eat. You can also grow snow or sugar peas and eat the tasty pods before the peas form.

Radishes grow very quickly and will be ready to eat three to four weeks after you plant them. Plant some radishes every week or two in the spring so you'll have fresh radishes for most of the summer.

Plant three or four pumpkin seeds in a mound in the centre of your garden. Pumpkin vines spread along the ground and take up a lot of space, but your radish and pea crops will be finished before the pumpkins take over your garden. If you plant the pumpkins in pots, let the vines trail on the ground around the pots. Pick your pumpkins in the fall when the skin is orange and hard.

A garden for wildlife

morning glory

hollyhock

Yarrow

dill

tobacco (Nicotiana)

parsley aster marigold

Grow some flowers for wildlife and enjoy the birds, butterflies and moths, and squirrels that come to visit. Plant the flowers in groups to make it easier for wildlife to find the food. If you don't have garden space, plant flowers in groups of pots in sunny areas.

Plant some morning glories, hollyhocks, fuchsias and Trumpet-creepers. In the summer, insects and hummingbirds will feed on the nectar of your flowers. The long, tubelike beak of a hummingbird is adapted for drinking nectar out of these trumpet- or bell-shaped flowers. Red and purple flowers attract the most hummingbirds.

Butterflies also sip nectar, but they need large, flat-topped flowers to land on and rest while they feed. Garden plants such as asters, Yarrow, parsley and dill attract a variety of butterflies. Moths usually feed in the evening and are attracted to flowers that are open then and that give off lots of perfume, such as ornamental tobacco (Nicotiana).

Trumpet-creeper

sunflower

tomato

cabbage broccoli carrot cauliflower

Don't pull up your plants when the flowers are finished blooming. Leave the dead plants in your garden all winter. Their seeds provide food for squirrels and birds, helping them survive the cold. Flowers that produce lots of seeds include sunflowers, zinnias, hollyhocks and marigolds.

Garden plants such as parsley, dill, carrots, cabbage, broccoli, cauliflower and tomatoes provide great places for butterflies and moths to lay their eggs. Check the leaves and stems of these plants for the eggs and caterpillars of these insects.

Index